coffee stains.

AF624509

Emma Burgess

BookLeaf Publishing

Presentation by *BookLeaf Publishing*

Web: www.bookleafpub.com

E-mail: info@bookleafpub.com

ISBN: 9789357213370

First edition 2023

cavity.

i could write of chocolate
or a flavour i still cannot decide
but coffee
it's addictive
+ the bitterness still fresh
in my cavity

you loved coffee.

you loved coffee
and although i drink coffee
it can be too bitter to me
i add too much sugar
diluting the full flavour
and though it reawakens me
and gives me energy to dance in the sun
i will still prefer tea

i love tea
so did you
but in the mornings
you would choose coffee
and watch me slowly sip
English breakfast at breakfast time
the coffee made you taste bitter
yet still i kissed you

even though i prefer tea

cold coffee.

the coffee
i've let it sit
for too long
it's getting cold
going stale
each sip a chore
unsatisfactory
sugar won't save it
warming it is just sad
but i'll keep sipping
            from this cup
            until someone stops me
            or i'm not poured any more

it's exhausting
forcing it down
like cough mixture
hoping each sip
will heal the burns
but it reopens them
plaguing scars
leaves me empty

lift me up
sweet caffeinated nectar

help me
warm me
energise me once more
i need you
i'm addicted to you
coffee
cof f e e
c o f f   e   e

but i know mum. i was never a coffee drinker.
you breathed into me a love for tea.
and i know tea will always heal me.

the blanket.

more than any other sense, smell is the most connected to memory. olfactory neurons generate an impulse passed along the olfactory nerve to areas connected to the olfactory bulb like the limbic system, which controls mood, emotion, behaviour and memory: primitive, emotional, sensual, memorable.

i've been meaning to wash it
it's been months
but i couldn't bring myself to
what if it ruins the soft
silky
touch
how it feels to wrap it
around myself
to warm me
to comfort me

but worse
it will lose the smell
the smell i suffocate myself with
because of the memories
the comfort
but now

it makes me tear up
it's burning my nostrils
inflaming my lungs
my throat is scratchy
                    putrid
                    rank
i let it sit
          unwashed
for too long

a comforting sip.

he called
hearing that voice
through the phone
made my heart leap
like muscle memory
for just a moment
          - old lovers, still friends

we talked like nothing
and everything happened
between us.
          - old lovers, soul friends

after you have seen the
entirety of someone
          their naked flesh
          the dark of their souls
can you ever not be friends
          - old lovers, best friends

i sipped for a moment
a comforting sip
          - no longer addicted to you

friends with an ex.

we sit
coffees in hand
staring
            or trying not to
tracing familiarity
talking about
what we never learned
of one another
            sipping
            laughing
            understanding
            transfiguring
                    love

phobia.

maybe it's not the commitment
that terrifies me
maybe it is the thought of
not being able to chase all of my dreams
with someone else's dreams to think of

let it burn.

pour the coffee over me
i don't care that it burns

let it

and may the scars remind me
of what it is to love
and not feel loved in return

crushed.

is it a crush or am i just alone, thinking about
nice people and imagining who they are and
what things could be?
is it a crush, or am i hungry and slightly
dehydrated?
is it a crush, or am i tired, cold and in need of a
hug?
is it a crush, or do i just want to spend time in
their company?
is it a crush, or was the conversation so delicious
i could talk and listen to them all day?
is it a crush, or have i found another soul to call
a friend?
is it a crush, or is it just something sticking with
me because of a joke someone said in passing?
is it a crush, or can i not stop thinking about
them because i am distracting myself from what
is right in front of me?
is it a crush, or is it a rebound?
is it a crush, or am i looking for an emotional
crutch?
is it a crush, or are they just wonderful to look
at?

is it as crush, or are they just a good human who
makes the world a little better every day just by
being in it?
is it a crush, or have i gone fucking insane?

ready.

i crave the burn
the rush
the rise in heart beat
how the heart yearns and aches
seared with each good bye
every time they turn away
i ache for that warmth
feeling so full in your chest
that you could be sick
and you can't breathe
or find words to describe
everything you feel
the pricking
the wholeness
the comfort and desire
i am ready for it all once more
to fall in love again

best supportive actress.

always the friend
not often the beauty
sometimes the smart
and always the sunshine in the room

until i am faded
disintegrated into the background
as yet another takes centre stage

always the sunshine
but never the star of the show

self-destruct.

i think what is destroying me
is that i know he is the one
that with him
all will be wonderful and chaotic and delicious
that breathing will be easy
and lying in the sun all day is not a waste of time

time
i don't want us to waste it
it is so precious
i should just tell him
as i doing everything
to ignore it

so i lay in the sun
catching my breath
wasting my time away
  our time away
trying to build myself for when we are ready
or to keep myself from collapsing in
on my screaming soul

losing it.

i think he has lost interest
perhaps there was never any there
maybe i am losing it too
i don't need the interest of others
i don't need a great love
i know i am wonderful
    and beautiful
    and loveable
but it wouldn't hurt
for someone else to see it
and tell me
that they are in love with it too

your greatest fear.

maybe it is not the commitment you are afraid of. but of being so vulnerable that you could get hurt. but maybe you should just go for it. you are never ready for something like this. it has caught you by surprise and you are afraid. you're afraid because they see you. they joke. they tease. but they look through all the shit and they see you. for the first time in your life you feel heard. seen. and it disrupts your soul because no one knows you like that. not even you. they see that there is darkness in there. that really you are afraid and hurting and underneath it all you just want to be loved for real. and maybe you haven't had great role models or maybe those around you have made you fear getting close. maybe you don't feel like you're enough. but you are. we all deserve the best. including you. and maybe you are the best for them. you've never opened your heart. it's hard work and it's terrifying. but you know this could be for real. and however afraid you are of going for it you are more afraid of potentially losing it. of letting it all slip away. letting this person that sees you more than anyone ever could – the hurt, the gentleness, the inner child – get away. you're terrified. that's how you know. this could be it. and you don’t think you’re ready. but are any of us ever really ready? does this stuff not just hit us when we least expect? when, maybe, we want it least? so is it better to not just sit with them. be with them. and go slowly? talk. exist together. be gentle. like you really are in your soul. and love. be loved. i know. you’re afraid now of hurting them too. but is this not the risk we take with our hearts? it hurts. all of it. a pain you did not expect to be so physical. but you need to trust. that's all we can ever do. trust and be gentle. and don’t let it slip away. not this one. not this time.

tell me.

tell me
tell me that you do
tell me that you know
tell me
tell me that you see it
tell me
say it
tell me that you love me
so i can tell you
that i love you

will they.

will they wake up one day and realise
it was me all along
will they be speaking to a friend
and suddenly just know
will we be with one another and with one look
never want to not sit beside me again
will they show up at my door
after pretending they could love another
will they watch me walk away
and then run out to grab me
to bring me back
because they suddenly do not care
about anything else in the world
if i'm not there to care with them
will they send me a message
after seeing a sunflower
because they know
it will make me smile
it made them think of me
will they sit on the couch
bathing in the afternoon sun
hand on my knee
just being

or will they never know
that some part of their soul
is without a crucial piece
and continue to float through life
never feeling quite right
because they never realised
they were in love with me

breaking our own hearts.

why is it so hard for us
to tell people that we love them
that we will make space for them
that we will embrace them always with open
arms?
is it not harder holding it in
and watching them chase another
because they do not know
how you truly feel?
why do we choose to break our own hearts
instead of opening them to each other?

# of course.

of course
you
who will not drink tea
or eat fruits with me
or smile at the sunset
or walk into the sea
you
the coffee drinker
you hurt me

aroma.

i can trace your smell
through my home
it lingers
sits
            on the air
in the spaces you filled
burning into my soul
brewing in my overthought
until i return home
and it is stale
and gone cold
until i breathe
your aroma again

indulgence.

her perfume
mingled with coffee on her breath
                    or tea aura
                    drinking it like water
she melts into the hard seat
softly smiling
melodies caught between her ears
watching rainforests
            seas
            rivers
            roads
                    f l o a t past her
skies transfiguring
thanking
        blessing
                herself
living this unreality
in her cautious way
indulging in earth
            air
            societies
flowing about her
falling into them
devouring culture
tasting + indulging

never nourishing curiosity
an e x p a n d i n g appetite
craving more
feeding the urges
        on buses
        on planes
her perfume
caffeinated breath
seeping into the atmosphere
bleeding into already red earth

coffee stains.

and so you loved coffee too
why do i keep falling
for the coffee lovers
leaving coffee stains
on my tea-loving heart

www.ingramcontent.com/pod-product-compliance
Lightning Source LLC
Chambersburg PA
CBHW051719130826
49812CB00034B/1254
* 9 7 8 9 3 5 7 2 1 3 3 7 0 *